52 Changes

52 Changes

Leo Babauta

WAKING LION PRESS

For my lovely children: Chloe, Justin, Rain, Maia, Seth and Noelle. I love you all immeasurably and boundlessly, without end.

ISBN 978-1-4341-0400-7

Published by Waking Lion Press, an imprint of The Editorium.

Waking Lion Press™, the Waking Lion Press logo, and The Editorium™ are trademarks of The Editorium, LLC.

The Editorium, LLC
West Jordan City, UT 84081-6132
Waking Lion Press.com
wakinglion@editorium.com

CONTENTS

HOW TO USE THIS BOOK

This is a book of 52 changes you can make in a year, one per week.

It's not meant to be read all at once. Instead, consider browsing through it but focusing on one small chapter per week. Open the book the following week and focus on a second chapter, and so on. We'll call it single-tasking.

You don't need to make all the changes in this book. You can easily pick 10 things, or 20, and focus on those, and do some of them for 2–3 weeks. You could pick 12 and do one per month.

Not all 52 apply to everyone. Some people aren't in debt and don't need the financial chapters. Just keep working on one of the other changes instead, or take a break.

However . . . if all 52 changes apply to you, feel free to do them all. You don't have to do them in this order, but it could be fun to give it a try.

This is a book of the 52 changes that I've made that I think matter most. Why are there exactly 52, instead of 45 or 73? It's a convenience—52 weeks in a year, 52 changes, one per week. I could have picked 12, but that would have been less fun!

INTRODUCTION

My name is Leo Babauta. You might know me as the creator of Zen Habits and someone who writes about simplicity and forming habits.

What makes me qualified to write this book? In short, I've transformed my life using some simple principles. I've learned how to make changes and have fun doing them. I do little experiments, one or two a month, and I see what happens. I stick with the changes that feel good, and leave behind those that don't work as well for me. That's what I suggest you do.

In the last 7 years (since 2005), I've made uncountable small changes—and yes, small changes are what work best. I started running, eventually running a marathon at the end of 2006 and two more in the next couple years, along with a number of other races and triathlons and the like. I started eating healthier, and am now a vegan, and have lost about 70 lbs.

I started waking earlier, meditating, learning to focus and stop procrastinating, paid off a lot of debt, started saving and then investing, created a popular website, wrote several books and created some popular courses, started traveling, moved my wife and six kids to San Francisco from Guam (whew! that was a biggie), gave up our second vehicle on Guam and then went car-free when we moved to San Francisco, and on and on.

I've made all the changes in this book at one time or another, though sometimes I have to revisit some of them. Yes, it's OK to let some of them go when it feels best for you, and revisit them when you feel up to it.

The changes in this book aren't a way to improve your life. Let me stress that: this isn't a self-improvement book. It's an experimentation book. It's a change lab. It's a way to explore yourself, to figure out what works best for you, to get out of your comfort zone, to learn how to change, and to be OK with change. And that's the most important thing: learning how to be OK with change.

It's about living life in a way that will give you the greatest fulfillment, will help you help the world, and to live more fully and in the present.

I present 52 Changes, with gratitude to you for reading it.

THE PRINCIPLES

One Change at a Time. Just one. Don't make several at once, because then they'll all fail.

Small Changes Only. Don't try to run 30 minutes if you haven't been running. Just do 2 minutes. Small changes are more likely to stick.

Enjoy the Change. If you don't enjoy it, it's not worth doing. And it won't stick anyway.

Iterate. If a change fails, figure out why, and improve the method. Or pick another change.

Pick a trigger. A trigger is something already ingrained in your routine that you use to anchor a new change. For example, go for a walk (the new habit) right after drinking coffee in the morning (the trigger).

Q: If I make a change one week, do I stick with it for the rest of the year? A: Yes, if it makes sense for you. Some changes are fundamental and can make powerful changes in your life, and you should keep these. But which changes are fundamental are different for each person—you'll know it when you feel it.

Q: but I can't possibly do 52 things a day, every day! How can I keep all the changes? A: You can't. Some changes will stick, others won't. Some changes you won't even attempt, because they might sound dumb or just not right for you. So do one of the other changes instead. Some changes you won't need to do every day—if you declutter a shelf, you just need to learn how to keep it decluttered, instead of doing it again every day. Even if it gets cluttered, you probably only need to do it once every few months.

Q: What do I do at the end of the year? A: You can review the changes you tried, see what worked best, see what you didn't stick with that you would like to try again. Go over the book again, and pick out ones to try again. Some of them you only want to do every 4–6 months anyway (clearing out a closet, for example).

CHANGE 1: MEDITATE

THE CHANGE: *Find a quiet place and sit for 2 minutes, focusing on your breathing. This is a simple form of meditation.*

WHY: Meditation is a way to practice mindfulness, which is a skill you can carry into your everyday life. When you're mindful, you are living in the present. You're more aware of your body, your thoughts, your emotional reactions, the people you're interacting with. You are less stressed, and more at peace. You are present in anything you do.

This mindfulness is the foundation for all the other changes in this book, so even if you feel silly trying it, I highly recommend you give it a try.

HOW:

Commit to just 2 minutes a day.

Pick a time and trigger.

Find a quiet spot. Sit comfortably.

Start with just 2 minutes.

Focus on your breath.

When you notice your mind wandering from the breath, just notice it and don't berate yourself or try to push away the thought, but gently return to the breath. Repeat this process as many times as you need to.

If you do well the first 2 or 3 days, feel free to expand to 5 minutes if it feels good. Otherwise, feel free to stay with 2 minutes the entire week. I recommend sticking to this 2–5 minutes a day for as long as you find it useful—possibly all year, or for the rest of your life. It's really essential practice. If you drop it for any reason, pick it up again later.

CHANGE 2: UNPROCRASTINATE

THE CHANGE: *Practice not procrastinating for just 10–15 minutes a day.*

WHY: Procrastination is one of the most common problems people have when they work—we know what we should be doing, but we put it off. That means we play games, go to time-wasting websites, check Facebook/Twitter and other social sites, check the news, check our email and other inboxes, do a bunch of busywork and smaller tasks . . . everything but the tasks we know we should be doing.

for example, I know I'm supposed to write this chapter today . . . and yet, I find a thousand smaller tasks to do before the actual writing, even though I know there's nothing more important than the writing. If I keep this up, my book will never get written!

Why do we do this? Because focusing on the important is often uncomfortable—difficult, unknown, unfamiliar, pushing beyond our comfort zone. We turn to what we're comfortable with. So we'll focus on getting comfortable with not procrastinating.

HOW:

Set aside some time every day for unprocrastination. Start with 5 minutes on Days 1 and 2, and 10 minutes on Days 3–7. Set it at a specific time—say 9 A.M.

Before your start time, have an important task picked out. Just one task. You only need to do the first 5 (or 10) minutes of it.

Clear distractions. Turn off the Internet, close all programs not needed, plug in some headphones and music if needed. Do all this before your start time.

When the start time comes, focus on just getting started. Nothing else in the world matters more than getting started at that time.

When you notice the urge to switch to something more comfortable, pause. Don't act, just watch. It's OK to have the urge, but what's important is learning that the urge doesn't control you. You can just watch it, even if that's a bit uncomfortable. Watch the urge, breathe, and then return to your important task.

Repeat the above step as many times as necessary.

Enjoy the process. When we dread something, we put it off—but instead, if we can learn to enjoy it, it won't be as hard or dreadful. Put yourself in the moment, and enjoy the task. Let go of the dread, and focus on the pleasantness, fun-ness, joy of the doing.

at the end of the 5–10 minutes, stop and go do something more comfortable. If you feel like repeating this during the day, feel free to do so. You're practicing being comfortable with unprocrastination, and as you do so, you're less likely to procrastinate. This takes practice, so feel free to continue this after the week is over.

CHANGE 3: WALK

THE CHANGE: *Take a 2–5 minute walk each day at a certain time. If you already are a good walker, feel free to do 10 minutes.*

WHY: Exercise is one of the most important things you can do, for your health and your mind. Walking is a great way to get moving while finding time to enjoy the outdoors.

If you already exercise, think of the walking as a bonus—it's better to exercise once a day and walk again later (or before the exercise session) than to exercise once and sit all day. Plus, it's a great way to let go of stress and find solitude for good thinking.

HOW:

Pick a time to do a short walk.

Commit to only 2–5 minutes, or 10 if you're a regular walker.

Focus on just getting out the door—starting is key.

Expand by 2–3 minutes a day.

a good way to enjoy the walking is to do it with someone else. Find a friend or family member (your partner, a best friend, your sibling or mom, etc.) and commit to walking each day at a certain time. If you know that you're meeting someone to go walking, you'll be more likely to show up, and you'll have more fun too. You can use this method for any of the habits in this book.

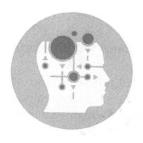

CHANGE 4: KEEP A FLEXIBLE MIND

THE CHANGE: *Learn to develop a flexible mind with small practices.*

WHY: the root cause of frustration, irritation, anger, sadness is an inflexible mind—one that wants to hold onto the way we wish things were, the ideas we're comfortable with. When things don't go this way, we are then frustrated, angry, sad.

So developing a flexible mind is a way to be open to anything, happy with change, prepared for any situation. Think about it: if there's a major disruption in your life, it's only a bad thing because you're holding onto the way you wish things could be, what you're comfortable with. If you let go of that wish, the change isn't bad. It's just different, and in fact it could be good if you embrace it and see the opportunity.

It's about developing the ability to cope with change, to be flexible, to simplify.

HOW:

Make a commitment, for one week, to try to let go of what you're holding onto when you get irritated, frustrated, sad, etc.

Make a list of the things that trigger these emotions—being interrupted, someone cutting you off in traffic, someone being loud when you're trying to work, people not washing their dishes, etc.

Create reminders for when those triggers happen—paper notes, a bead bracelet, something written on your hand, a sign on your car's dashboard, etc.

When the trigger happens, pause. Notice the emotion rising. Feel it, but don't act. Breathe.

Try to see what you're holding onto—wishing the driver would be more polite, wishing you could do what you were doing without interruptions, wishing other people would be perfect in cleaning up after themselves. These wishes are fantasies—let them go. Be open to the way things are, to changes that have happened. Breathe, open your heart, accept.

Now respond appropriately, without wishing things were different, with compassion.

Repeat however many times you like during the week, or a minimum of once a day.

Please note that you will not be perfect at this when you start. It's a difficult skill to learn, because we have emotional patterns that have built up over the years. It's good enough to become more aware of it, and to attempt this method once a day. Be flexible in your desire to get this exactly right. Practice it when you remember for the rest of the year.

CHANGE 5: IDENTIFY YOUR ESSENTIALS

THE CHANGE: *Make a short list of the things that are most important to you.*

WHY: the first rule of simplifying is to identify the essential, what you love, what is important to you—and then cut out all the rest that distracts you and keeps you from doing what's important. We have so much stuff in our lives, from possessions to things we need to do to information coming in to visual and emotional clutter, that we are overloaded. The result? We end up doing a lot of things that aren't really important to us, because we have so much other stuff to do that has crept into our lives and that we leave in our lives, unexamined.

HOW:

on Day 1 of this week, make a list of all the things you do in your life, all your commitments, as well as the things you wish you did (things you really love but don't have time for). This is your long list.

on Day 2, pick the top 4–5 things from the long list. Just the things you love most. This is your short list. (My short list: writing/helping people, reading, running/exercise, and my family. Not in that order.)

on Day 3, figure out which of the things you do these days are on your short list, and which aren't.

on Day 4, consider sending an email or making a call to get out of something that you do that isn't on your short list, even if it seems fairly important. Will life go on if you cancel the commitment? Is it worth canceling so that you can have space for your short list items?

on Day 5, schedule a block of time in your calendar for something that's on your short list that you don't have enough time for. Consider this appointment sacred.

and you can continue this process in the coming weeks—begin to eliminate or reduce the things that aren't on your short list to make room for those that are. Schedule time for the things on your short list.

Simplifying isn't meant to leave your life empty—it's meant to leave space in your life for what you really want to do. Know what those things are before you start simplifying.

CHANGE 6: EAT MINDFULLY

THE CHANGE: *Practice eating mindfully.*

WHY: Often our overeating issues are caused by emotional triggers and the resulting mindless eating. We eat for emotional reasons—for comfort, as a reward, because of loneliness or stress or boredom. Mindful eating helps us to become aware of these triggers, and to separate them from the actual eating.

Mindful eating also helps us to eat more slowly, to savor the food instead of scarfing it down, to enjoy it more fully. You're also sated with less food, and don't eat too much.

HOW:

Choose one meal each day and commit to focusing on mindful eating at that meal, every day for a week.

at the chosen meal, single-task. Don't look at your mobile device, or your computer, or the TV. Don't read or have any kind of entertainment. Just eat.

Have a designated place to eat. At the table, with nothing else but a glass of water or cup of tea.

Look at the food. Enjoy the beauty of the thing you are about to eat.

Savor each mouthful. Chew it slowly and taste it fully. Enjoy the flavors, the textures. One bite at a time. Swallow and pause for a breath before even considering to scoop up another bite.

Notice your emotional triggers when you are about to eat, and during the eating.

When you are almost sated, pause for about 5 minutes. See if you're full. Go do something else, and only eat more if you are still hungry after 5–10 minutes.

Continue to practice this throughout the year. You can do it in social situations, and at parties you can indulge without guilt, because you'll eat a smaller amount, but slowly.

CHANGE 7: DO THE MOST IMPORTANT THINGS (MITs)

THE CHANGE: *Pick 1–3 things each morning as the most important things you can get done today. These are your MITs. There might only be one of them. Focus on doing the first one first, before starting anything else in your workday.*

WHY: We often get caught up in small tasks, busywork that lets us feel productive while the most important tasks get pushed back later and later, until we don't have time to do them anymore because of all the smaller "urgent" things that come up. This is a form of procrastination, or at least bad priorities.

As an example, if you're a writer who needs to write a book, you might put off the writing until after checking email, which generates a dozen other small tasks that need to be taken care of, then perhaps there's a meeting or two, or an errand to take care of, then something comes up that needs to be fixed immediately, then you're too tired to write or the day is over. Instead, what if you wrote the chapter before doing anything else? The other stuff would get figured out, but the most important thing would get done.

HOW:

Each morning (or the evening before), pick at least 1 MIT (3 at the most). Try to limit them to 20–30 minute tasks, or break them into smaller ones if they take longer than 20–30 minutes. For example, if you want to write a book chapter but can't do it in 20–30 minutes, just write a page or half page.

Getting the task finished isn't as important as doing 20–30 minutes of it—you can keep going when you get to that point, but you don't need to continue.

Before you do anything else for work (including checking email), do the first MIT. Block out distractions, and just focus on starting.

When you get that done, celebrate! Take a break, stretch, maybe give yourself 10 minutes of email or other busywork, then get started on the 2nd MIT. Starting is the key.

CHANGE 8: CLEAR A SHELF

THE CHANGE: *Declutter one or more shelves or flat spaces in your house or work space.*

WHY: a decluttered space feels peaceful, while lots of physical clutter is a form of visual distraction. Decluttering your entire home or office at once is too overwhelming for most people, so we'll start with one or more flat surfaces, such as shelves, countertops or tables. Once you get started, you might want to keep going!

HOW:

Pick one shelf or other flat surface (counter, table, etc.). Set aside 10 minutes or so to work on this space.

Clear the entire shelf or space. Take everything off, put it in a pile or a small area on the floor. Get two boxes for sorting.

Go through the pile of stuff one item at a time. The rule is, you can't skip an item or put it back. You have to decide what to do with it immediately, quickly! See next step.

Make a quick decision on the item—you have three choices and must separate things into three groups: the keep pile only if you love it or use it often; the donate box (or trash bag)—dispose of those asap; and the maybe box, where you absolutely can't bear to part with something you don't need or use. Try not to use the maybe box unless you're truly stuck on an item.

the maybe box, if you need it, should be marked with a date six months from now, and a reminder should be put on that date on your calendar.

When that date comes, if you haven't used the items in the maybe box by then, donate them. You didn't need them.

Put the "keep" items back on the shelf, or in another more appropriate place perhaps. Wherever you put them is important—this is the item's new home, and you should always put the item back in that home when you're done using it.

If you don't finish the shelf in 10 minutes, feel free to go a little longer if you have the time or energy, or continue to work on it for another 10 minutes the next day, and so on until you're done.

Once you've finished with that shelf, feel free to pick another shelf, table, countertop, closet floor or other flat space. Declutter one flat space at a time.

CHANGE 9: START SAVING

THE CHANGE: *Create a small emergency fund savings account if you haven't yet. If you already have a decent savings and are out of debt, consider starting to invest.*

WHY: One of the most important things you can do when you're getting your financial house in order is to create an emergency fund. It's really hard to consistently pay off debt if you have zero savings.

a savings account will help you smooth out your finances—when an emergency comes up, like your car breaking down or someone having to go to the hospital, you won't be thrown back into indebtedness. You will have some cash to pay for that emergency, and you can use your regular paycheck for regular expenses.

HOW:

Set up a savings account if you don't have one yet. It's fairly simple to set up a high-yield online savings account such as EmigrantDirect. This kind of fund is good because you can't just spend from it when you have an immediate urge to buy something, but you can get funds within 2–3 days if there's a strong need.

Begin depositing into it regularly, at least $50 per paycheck while you're in debt if finances are very tight, then $100 when you have a little more breathing room, but more if you can.

If you can't find $50 or $100 per payday, take a hard look at your spending. There's usually something you can cut back on: cell phone or Internet or cable bill, magazines or newspapers (read for free online), books (get them from a library), Netflix or other online services, movies and going out, alcohol, Starbucks drinks, restaurants, shopping, buying treats like sweets or chips or sodas, new clothes, travel, an extra vehicle, parties, gifts, new equipment or gadgets, a gym membership (work out at home), cigarettes or other drugs, toys, a coach or classes, etc. Alternatively, you can find creative ways to earn additional income to save the $50 to $100 as well.

Set up an automatic transfer to your savings every payday. Make this your first bill to pay. If you already have a decent emergency fund (say two months' living expenses), look into investing, increase your 401K contributions, open an IRA, or invest in an index fund such as the Vanguard 500. Make it a regular and automatic contribution. The retirement investments are good vehicles because, by law, they're tax deferred, which means you're paying less in taxes and using that to make more money through investments.

If you're already doing all this, consider setting up your bills to pay automatically. I've done this for a few years now and never worry about bills anymore.

Change 10: Start Yoga or Strength Training

THE CHANGE: *Commit to just 2–5 minutes of yoga or bodyweight strength training each day this week.*

WHY: Exercise has so many important benefits that they can't all be listed, but they include more physical strength, better physical appearance, better heart and respiratory health, staving off diseases of all kinds, better mental health, less stress, better memory, better focus and much more.

Yoga is one of the most minimal of exercises, in that you can do it anywhere, wearing pretty much anything (though comfortable clothes that allow you to stretch is preferred), and it helps you to get stronger, fitter, more flexible, and more mindful, present and focused. I highly recommend it.

Strength training has many of the same benefits—it helps you get stronger and more confident, healthy, focused and feeling great. It's not just for men, either—women benefit immensely from strength training and shouldn't be intimidated (not that you are—but some women avoid it). I recommend you start with bodyweight strength exercises—weights are good for progressing after you've done bodyweight exercises for awhile.

I'm recommending both this week, not because you should do both at the same time (you can but shouldn't start that way), but to give you some choice. Some people don't like the idea of doing yoga, so you should do bodyweight exercises. Some don't like strength training of any kind, so you should do yoga. However, I really do recommend you try both eventually.

HOW:

You don't need any extra equipment for either of these activities, nor new clothes. You can do both on the floor of your living room, outside on grass, next to your desk, anywhere you can lay down and stretch your arms. You can wear yoga or workout clothes if you like, but don't go out and buy any if you don't have them. I like to wear loose shorts and a tank top or T-shirt, but have done strength training in jeans before.

Set aside just 2 minutes the first two days for either yoga or strength training. Find a clear space on a floor where you can work out. Pick a time during the day to do it. In the morning, or right after work, are two of my favorite times.

If you're doing yoga: pick one or two poses to try—do a Youtube search for instructions. You don't need a DVD at this point.

If you're doing strength training, I recommend the pushup, squat and pullup to start with. Start with just one of these the first day, and do what you can. If you can't do pushups, do them on your knees, or try wall pushups (leaning against a wall, or a sturdy table or counter). If you can't fully squat, just do it partially. If you can't do a pullup (most can't), use a chair to get yourself up and just lower yourself with resistance. Do a set that's less than the max you can do, rest a minute, then try another set.

on Day 2, do another 2 minutes. On Day 3 and 4, feel free to expand to 5 minutes. If you're feeling good on Day 5, expand to 7 minutes. But never feel the need to go longer if you're not feeling good about it—at this point, it's much more important that you continue do it than going longer. Form the habit first, and don't worry about results at this point.

After this week, consider continuing the habit for the rest of the year. If you do, feel free to try new yoga poses, new strength exercises (the lunge, burpees, the plank), and switch between strength and yoga. They compliment each other well.

After a couple months, if strength training is getting easier, feel free to add some weights—dumbbells, a barbell, a sandbag, a kettlebell. For yoga, you might try a yoga DVD or class.

a note: While starting new exercise can feel uncomfortable, it shouldn't be painful. You should be able to push past your comfort zone a little, because if we only do what's comfortable, we'll never make meaningful changes. However, again, you don't want to do something that's truly painful—it's a sign that you're injured or you're doing it wrong.

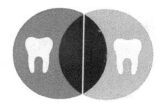

CHANGE 11: FLOSS

THE CHANGE: *Take 2 minutes to floss every evening.*

WHY: It's one of the most overlooked activities when it comes to being healthy and taking care of ourselves. We all brush our teeth (I hope) because otherwise our breath will smell bad and it's embarrassing. But no one (except your dentist) knows if you flossed. That's the wrong attitude—your teeth will decay and eventually you'll have very bad dental health, or you'll have to pay for expensive (and painful) dental work.

I only started flossing regularly in 2012, I'm embarrassed to say. But I've found that flossing can fairly quickly improve your dental health. If you haven't been flossing, it's likely that you have some kind of gum infection, and so flossing will cause some unpleasant (but not really painful) bleeding. That's normal, and it will go away after a few days of flossing (at least in my experience).

Your teeth will also start to feel cleaner, which is an amazing experience. And when you go to the dentist (if you aren't regularly, you should, trust me), you'll get a much better report, and have much less nasty dental work to be done.

HOW:

Pick a trigger in the evening before bedtime. For a habit to be automatic, it needs a trigger—something that is already in your daily routine. What do you normally do before bed? (Note: if the evening absolutely doesn't work for you, because you're too tired to create a new habit, do it in the morning when you brush your teeth.)

Have a visual reminder. The key is to do the new habit right after the trigger, but at first you might easily forget. So have the dental floss right next to your toothbrush, where you won't forget it. You might also put up a note next to your bathroom mirror so you can't possibly forget.

Just do a minute the first day. You don't have to be thorough—you're trying to form the habit, not give yourself a full-on cleaning. Don't be overzealous.

Slowly expand each day, until you're getting all your teeth. It'll get easier, and less painful. Enjoy the feeling of clean teeth.

If you don't already, consider a fluoride rinse after you floss and brush at night. The feeling of a clean mouth as you go to bed is one of the little secrets of life.

Consider keeping this habit for the rest of the year as well. It's a great one to have, and only takes a couple minutes each night.

CHANGE 12: PAY A SMALL DEBT

THE CHANGE: *If you have debt, and aren't already on a serious plan to pay it off, get started by paying a small debt.*

WHY: Debt can be crippling if it overwhelms you and eats up your income with payments owed and high interest. It can be limiting, stopping you from doing what you want to do. It can be hugely stressful.

One of the best changes I've made is learning to spend less than I earn, which seems like such a basic concept except so few of us do it. Paying off my debt (something that took 2 years to do) and staying debt-free has made me so much freer, so much less worried about finances.

However, it can be overwhelming to tackle a large amount of debt—I personally avoided it because of this feeling of dread. So we'll tackle it in baby steps.

HOW:

on Day 1, simply start a list of all your debts. Don't worry about the amounts—just things you owe money on. Don't worry about getting the list complete—just start. You might list your credit cards, auto loan(s), student loan(s), mortgage, medical debts, friends and family you owe, etc.

on Day 2, if you haven't yet, finish the list. Start to look up the amounts and add them to the list.

on Day 3, finish looking up and writing down the amounts of the debt. If you can't find an amount, make a guess. Now put the list in order, from smallest to largest.

on Day 4, pick the smallest debt. This is your first target. You'll pay this debt first before worrying about the others. Pay the minimum you can pay on all other debts, including zero if you can avoid penalties. If you pay all your bills and the minimum on everything else, what's the max you can pay on this first, small debt? Write down a number for now.

on Day 5, take a look at cutting back. If you don't have any extra, take a look at your discretionary spending. Can you commit to spending less on eating out, going to the movies, shopping, buying clothes and gadgets, at least for now? Can you cancel one of your cell phone plans or drop to a lower plan for cell or Internet usage? Can you cancel subscriptions to cable TV, Netflix, magazines, online services you might be paying for? Alternatively, is there a way to earn additional money outside your job? Could you clean houses, mow lawns, pet sit, or perform some other valuable service? Find the extra cash, and commit to temporarily cutting back or eliminating while you're paying off debt.

on Day 6, make a payment to the target debt. If you normally pay $25, and you're committing to an extra $50 or $100 (or whatever), pay the extra amount today—online if possible, or in person if needed. Many banks have electronic bill pay services you can use, if the debt you're paying doesn't have a way to accept online payments. See if you can set up a recurring payment in the larger amount for your target debt, until the debt is paid off.

Rest on Day 7

Celebrate. (Not by buying something though!) Often a smaller debt can be paid off immediately (if you've cut back on stuff) or in a few months. However long it takes, once you're done, take the entire amount you were paying on that target debt, and apply it to the next largest debt on your list. Example: You were paying $75/month on Debt 1 (and $100 on Debt 2), then paid Debt 1 off in 3 months . . . take the $75 from Debt 1 and apply it to Debt

So now you'll be paying $175/month on Debt

Once Debt 2 is paid off, you'll apply that $175 to whatever you're paying on Debt 3, and so on.

Also, don't take on new debt if you can avoid it! Cut back on your spending so that you begin to live within your means.

CHANGE 13: EXERCISE MINDFULLY

THE CHANGE: *Use simple exercise as mindfulness practice.*

WHY: Many people dread exercise because they see it as hard, boring, a chore, or drudgery that they have to get through but would rather not. This is the opposite of how you should view exercise—it's a form of meditation, an enjoyable experience that helps teach you how to be present.

Many people also think they don't have time for this "luxury", but in truth, regular exercise is one of the most important changes you can make. It's just as important as brushing your teeth everyday, more important than watching TV or reading online or answering email. Make time for something so crucial to a good life.

While I love meditation, it's only one way to practice mindfulness. Exercise is another good practice—it can be a beautiful, calming activity if you focus on being mindful.

HOW:

If you're not already doing yoga or strength training, commit to just 2 minutes of mindful exercise a day. Pick a certain time, like right after your morning coffee, or right after leaving work. If you're already doing yoga, just practice focusing on mindfulness as you do it (you're supposed to be doing that anyway), and increase the time you do it by 2 minutes. If you're already doing strength training, use this as mindfulness practice.

Other than yoga/strength training, good choices for exercise include walking, running, hiking, tai chi, swimming, and the like. It's probably best to choose something you're already familiar with, and if you're not familiar with any of them, choose walking.

As you start, take a deep breath, paying attention to the sensations of the breath as it comes in, and then as it goes out. You can do this a few times, but after that, just breath normally but pay attention to the breath as you exercise.

from your breath, you can also pay attention to your body as it moves. Notice the sensations of the muscles and joints, of wind as it blows on your body, of sunlight.

Notice also your mind, as thoughts come up that pull you from focusing on your body and breath. Don't try to squash these thoughts or push them away, but notice them, then gently return to the breath and body.

Just do 2 minutes at first. If you enjoy it, increase it to 5 minutes after 3–4 days.

This is another good habit to keep for the rest of the year. The focus of this habit is not on getting fit or trim or buff, but on practicing mindfulness. This practice can then be carried to the rest of your day.

Change 14: Budget Simply

THE CHANGE: *Create a simple budget and system to follow it, if you don't have one already.*

WHY: This is something many people put off, because it seems so difficult. But it's not, really. It can be simple, and it helps you get your finances straight. A budget is simply a plan, a tool for figuring out where your money should go instead of it just slipping through your fingers on a regular basis.

You don't need to stick religiously to a budget for the rest of your life, but if your finances aren't as good as they should be, use this to help get yourself in shape. Once you're there, you can put things on autopilot and not really think about it much.

HOW:

Set up a simple spreadsheet. In one column, list your monthly bills (rent or mortgage, auto payment, other debt payments, utilities, cable, etc.)— everything that is a regular monthly expense. Then list variable expenses (things that change every month) like groceries, gas, eating out, etc. Later you should add irregular expenses (stuff that comes up once in awhile— less than once a month) such as auto and house maintenance, clothing, insurance, etc. But we won't get into that now, as we want to keep it simple.

in the second column, put down the amounts for each. Be sure to put enough for things like gas and groceries, as you don't want to be short. Be sure to also include your minimum debt payments and your emergency fund deposit.

Now, list your income sources as monthly amounts. Use the spreadsheet's "SUM" feature to add up the totals in the columns. There. You've got a temporary spending plan (you'll want to add the irregular expenses later). Now, if the expenses are greater than the income, you'll need to make adjustments until the expenses are equal to or less than the income.

Income should be streamed into your checking account automatically. Most people get their income electronically these days I think. In a couple cases I've purposely set up electronic payments when previously I was sent checks.

Set up bill payments, debt payments, savings & investments so that they're automatically taken from your checking account. If it's not automatic, you might forget about it. Set a calendar reminder to check on how things are going each month.

Simplify: see what "mandatory" payments you can eliminate. This might take time, but many things are optional. For example, I eliminated cable TV, magazine subscriptions, a car payment (going from two cars to one), and more. Also, see what discretionary spending you can eliminate while you're trying to reduce debt—Starbucks coffee, eating out a lot, buying magazines or comics, etc.

What's left over is spending cash. Maybe it's for groceries, gas, and fun money (eating out, movies etc.). If you have difficulty not spending your grocery and gas money so that they last for two weeks, put the amounts you think you'll need in separate envelopes—one for gas, one for groceries, one for fun money.

CHANGE 15: CREATE A SUPPORT CREW

THE CHANGE: *Gather a group of people around you who will help you make your changes, cheer you on, and hold you accountable.*

WHY: Actually we probably should have made this one of the first changes, because as you might know by now, it's difficult to make changes if the people around you actively oppose you. I didn't put this earlier in the book because it's not as sexy, and many people will skip it if it's one of the first changes listed.

However, if you've found change to be difficult without a group of supportive people around you, this week we'll start to fix that. Sometimes you get lucky, and your spouse or family or friends (or all of them) are immediately on board with any changes you want to make, and root you on the whole way. Often, though, we're not so lucky: significant others can resist our changes, they can feel threatened and actively oppose us in various ways. That's difficult. Let's look at some ways to fix this.

HOW:

Start conversations with the important people around you. Your significant other, kids, parents, siblings, other close family members, best friends, close co-workers. These people would be invaluable to be on your team. Start by explaining what you've been doing, why, and why it's important to you. Tell them you really could use their support, ask for their help. This often works.

Join an online community. Find other people online who are making the same changes. I've joined communities of people who are quitting smoking, running, vegan, simplifying, getting fit, losing weight, and more. There's a group out there for any change. Sometimes influential blogs have good communities—spend some time looking around, then introduce yourself, get to know people, ask for help, offer help, find accountability partners.

Find passionate people in your town. Many people don't believe change is possible because everyone around them is stuck, living unhealthy lives, doing work they don't enjoy, not able to change their habits. But if you find people who not only believe it's possible, but are making the same changes you're looking to make, then your world changes. Look for these people—once your eyes are open, you'll find them. They're at 5K races, homeschooling groups, gyms and climbing walls, hiking on trails, participating in National Novel Writing Month (NaNoWriMo), blogging about local happenings, in vegan groups, and so forth. Find them, and make friends.

Passion and change are contagious. Find the people who are living these values, and surround yourself with them.

CHANGE 16: EAT SOME VEGGIES

THE CHANGE: *Add some veggies to your diet, once a day.*

WHY: Many people eat few if any vegetables, often because they don't like the taste or think of them as bland or yucky tasting. Veggies are often an afterthought—some wilted iceberg lettuce, perhaps.

but vegetables are nutritional powerhouses—there's nothing more important that you can add to your diet (nuts, beans and legumes, seeds, whole grains are other good additions). They pack an amazing nutritional punch for the amount of calories they have—50–100 calories of green or orange veggies, for example, can give you a ton of iron, Vitamin a, calcium, fiber and much more.

If you want to lose weight, or just maintain weight without gaining fat over the years, adding veggies and removing some high-calorie fatty foods or empty white carbs is the best way to do it. But first we have to learn to love veggies for the delicious superfoods they are.

HOW:

Pick one meal a day (say, lunch or dinner) and commit to adding one veggie to that meal each day this week. The ideas for each day are just ideas—if you want to mix it up or try your own thing, go for it.

on Day 1, just add some carrots. Most people like them. Dipping them in hummus is a fun way to make them tasty.

on Day 2, try some baked sweet potato or squash. These are delicious veggies with color and vitamins and a bit of sweetness to make them more palatable.

on Day 3, add a side salad to your meal—some leafy greens (not iceberg lettuce), maybe some shredded carrot and raw almonds/walnuts, a couple slices of avocado perhaps, any other veggies that sound good. Mix together a little balsamic vinegar and olive oil and ground black pepper and sprinkle it on the salad for flavor.

on Day 4, dice up a bunch of kale and put it in soup, chili, spaghetti sauce, or another dish you like where it won't overwhelm you with its strong flavor.

on Day 5, sauté some broccoli with olive oil and garlic until it's just a little browned. Add a little salt and pepper, and eat this as a side dish with your main meal.

on Day 6, sauté some kale or spinach or chard with olive oil and garlic. Add lemon juice, red pepper flakes, and a sprinkle of tamari or soy sauce.

on Day 7, get crazy—cook up a stir-fry with 3–4 different veggies. For example, cube some tempeh, tofu, seitan, or chicken, and cook it with canola oil and diced onions and garlic. Once the protein is a bit cooked, add some chopped veggies—broccoli, carrots, snow peas, greens, mushrooms, and more can all work. Add some Asian-inspired sauce, like teriyaki or oyster sauce or just tamari/soy sauce with mirin or rice vinegar or sesame oil. There are lots of recipes online for stir-frys if you don't feel like making it up yourself.

There are lots of other fun ways to incorporate veggies into your diet—eat a big salad (lots of veggies with beans, nuts, seeds, maybe some protein and feta cheese), pile veggies on a sandwich, make a lentil and carrot soup with greens, experiment!

I highly recommend you continue to expand veggies in your diet for the rest of the year.

CHANGE 17: CULTIVATE GRATITUDE

THE CHANGE: *Practice a gratitude ritual each day.*

WHY: Gratitude is one of the best ways to find contentment. We are often discontent in our lives, desire more, because we don't realize how much we have. Instead of focusing on what you don't have, be grateful for the amazing gifts you've been given: of loved ones and simple pleasures, of health and sight and the gift of music and books, of nature and beauty and the ability to create, and everything in between. Be grateful every day.

Gratitude reminds you of the positive things in your life. It makes you happy about the people in your life, whether they're loved ones or just a stranger you met who was kind to you in some ways.

Gratitude turns bad things into good things. Having problems at work? Be grateful you have work. Be grateful you have challenges, and that life isn't boring. Be grateful that you can learn from these challenges. Be thankful they make you a stronger person.

Gratitude reminds you of what's important. It's hard to complain about the little things when you give thanks that your children are alive and healthy. It's hard to get stressed out over paying bills when you are grateful there is a roof over your head.

HOW:

Commit to a 2-minute gratitude session each morning (or right before you go to bed).

Simply sit in a spot with no distractions, close your eyes, and think about what you're grateful for and who you're grateful for. Then smile.

Also take a second to give thanks for "negative" things in your life. There are always two ways to look at something. Many times we think of something as negative—it's stressful, harmful, sad, unfortunate, difficult. But that same thing can be looked at in a more positive way. Giving thanks for those things is a great way to remind yourself that there is good in just about everything. Problems can be seen as opportunities to grow, to be creative.

Say thank you—when someone does something nice for you, however small, try to remember to say thank you. And really mean it.

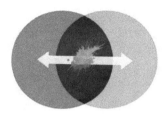

CHANGE 18: CLEAR COUNTERS

THE CHANGE: *Clear the counters in your home, and learn to keep them clear.*

WHY: We started clearing shelves and other flat spaces earlier, and found the peace that comes from a decluttered space. We're going to continue that with counters.

Counters are a large parts of our kitchens and other rooms in our homes—having clear counters will be a nice way to make a house feel clear and enjoyable.

Even if you cleared a counter or two in our earlier decultttering week (Change 7: Clear a shelf), it might be getting cluttered again by now. That's OK. We just need to learn a couple habits that will help keep them clear and beautiful from now on.

HOW:

Start with the same method as the "clear a shelf" week—pick one counter to start with. Clear it off and put everything on the ground in one big pile, and get two boxes for sorting

Go through the pile of stuff one item at a time. The rule is, you can't skip an item or put it back. Make a quick decision on the item—you have three choices and must separate things into three groups: 1) the keep pile—only if you love it or use it often, 2) the donate box (or trash bag)—dispose of those as soon as possible, and 3) the maybe box, where you absolutely can't bear to part with something you don't need or use. Try not to use the maybe box unless you're truly stuck on an item.

Put the "keep" items back on the counter, or in another more appropriate place perhaps. Wherever you put them is important—this is the item's new home, and you should always put the item back in that home when you're done using it.

Now here's the long-term habit part: be very conscious for the rest of the week about putting items only in their homes. Instead of tossing something on the counter, find a spot for it—it should have a home, or if it doesn't, create one.

by getting into the habit of putting things back, rather than tossing them randomly on the counter, you'll keep the counter clear. Find a home for something, and always put it there—those are the two little habits to create.

If you have time, do another counter, and so on until all your counters are clear!

CHANGE 19: SLOW DOWN

THE CHANGE: *Practice moving at a slower pace for a small time each day.*

WHY: Our lives are faster-paced and more hectic than ever before. Life moves at such a fast pace that it seems to pass us by before we can really enjoy it.

However, it doesn't have to be this way. Let's rebel against a hectic lifestyle and slow down to enjoy life.

a slower-paced life means making time to enjoy your mornings, instead of rushing off to work in a frenzy. It means taking time to enjoy whatever you're doing, to appreciate the outdoors, to actually focus on whoever you're talking to or spending time with—instead of always being connected to an iPhone or laptop, instead of always thinking about work tasks and emails. It means single-tasking rather than switching between a multitude of tasks and focusing on none of them.

Slowing down is a conscious choice, and not always an easy one, but it leads to a greater appreciation for life and a greater level of happiness.

HOW:

Schedule a block of time each day for doing less. Just 10 minutes the first day or two, but try to expand it to 20 and then 30 if you can.

Disconnect. Don't always be connected. Close your browser and/or turn off the computer. If you carry around an iPhone or other mobile device, shut it off. Better yet, learn to leave it behind when possible. Being connected all the time means we're subject to interruptions, we're constantly stressed about information coming in, we are at the mercy of the demands of others. It's hard to slow down when you're always checking new messages coming in.

Do less. It's hard to slow down when you are trying to do a million things. Instead, make the conscious choice to do less. Focus on what's really important, and let go of the rest. Put space between tasks and appointments, so you can move through your days at a more leisurely pace. Read more. Try doing nothing for a little while.

Be present. It's not enough to just slow down—you need to actually be mindful of whatever you're doing at the moment. That means, when you find yourself thinking about something you need to do, or something that's already happened, or something that might happen . . . gently bring yourself back to the present moment. Focus on what's going on right now. On your actions, on your environment, on others around you. This takes practice but is essential.

Breathe. When you find yourself speeding up and stressing out, pause, and take a deep breath. Take a couple more. Really feel the air coming into your body, and feel the stress going out. By fully focusing on each breath, you bring yourself back to the present, and slow yourself down. It's also nice to take a deep breath or two—do it now and see what I mean.

CHANGE 20: PLAY

THE CHANGE: *Incorporate play into your daily routine.*

WHY: When we approach everything as a form of playing, then everything we do can be fun. Nothing is boring, drudgery, tedious.

It's a matter of remembering what it was like to be a child. Take my 6-year-old daughter Noelle as an example. Everything she does becomes a game, an opportunity for wonder and exploration, or at the very least an opportunity to sing a song. She's never bored. Why is that?

Because she doesn't see anything as boring. Everything is new, and there's always a game you can play.

We can do that too. Every chore can be turned into play. Every walk to the store can be infused with a beginner's mind, so that we see our surroundings afresh, ripe for exploration. Every boring work task can be turned into a challenge, a game.

My 8-year-old son Seth runs everywhere, jumps everywhere. We're walking along the street and he's a werewolf, a wizard, a superhero. A living room becomes a place to make a fort, styrofoam becomes a toy, and if there's nothing to play with, he's pacing around making up stories in his head. How can you ever be bored when you see life like this?

HOW:

Pick a 10-minute spot in your workday, and mark it on your calendar as play. Actually, any activity can be play, but we often get bored with work tasks, so let's infuse play into work.

During this 10-minute spot, see what you can do to turn your current work task into play. There are lots of ideas: sing as you do it, give yourself a challenge, give yourself points for doing different things, imagine you're in a movie when you walk into a meeting, dance, see how fast you can do something, pretend you're a wizard, pretend everyone around you is a vampire, call your co-workers "Jeeves", talk to your computer and give it a name, do a victory dance when you finish something, pretend you're new at whatever you're doing and you've never done it before.

I can't stress the importance of work as play enough. It has turned my life into something joyful, it's allowed me to create and accomplish so much more than ever before, and I love every minute of it. I wish you nothing less than this simple happiness.

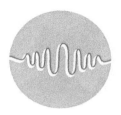

CHANGE 21: FLOW

THE CHANGE: *Create a focus zone for your most important work each day.*

WHY: Flow is a state where you lose yourself in a task, forgetting about the world around you as you are completely immersed in what you're doing. Finding focus and getting into flow is a way to stop ourselves from falling victim to the trap of the Internet—a wonderful empowering tool that can fill your day with distractions, a million little "productive" tasks that don't matter, constant interruptions from messages and status updates.

Who doesn't fall victim to this?

We are frittering our lives away.

HOW:

Set a "focus zone" each day—start with 10 minutes. If you're still doing the unprocrastination habit, you can use this as your focus zone, but perhaps extend it by 10 minutes.

During this time, turn off the Internet and close your browser, email program, and anything else you normally communicate and/or read with. Turn off notifications and your phone/mobile device. Have a challenging but enjoyable task to work on—I like to focus on writing, but other creative tasks are also great.

Learn to get into the "flow" of the task. This means immersing yourself in the task, letting the world around you fade away as you lose yourself in the doing. It's a form of meditation, and it takes practice. Often we have short attention span disorder, wanting to switch from one task to another, but during your focus zone, you'll practice sticking to the task, and really getting into it.

You only need to do this for 10 minutes at first—or just 5 minutes if 10 is too difficult. Slowly expand your focus zone by 5 minutes every few days, until you're doing somewhere between 30–60 minutes at a time, taking breaks in between (it's not good to do 4 hours at a time, as you need to be able to move, breathe, and take mental breaks). Feel free to stick to this habit and create 2–4 focus zones a day.

Change 22: Let Go of a Vice

THE CHANGE: *Let go of a bad habit such as smoking, drinking, fried foods, soda, shopping, porn, etc. for a week.*

WHY: We know that these bad habits are not good for us—but they're hard to control, and in truth, many times we don't want to quit. We enjoy them too much!

These bad habits fill a genuine need—they are ways to cope with stress, or to give ourselves pleasure, reward, comfort, love. We've all done it, so I'm not judging, but I view these things as negative coping.

Again, I've done many of these bad habits, so I know that they can feel like you're really de-stressing . . . but in fact, they can actually lead to more stress. Eating, smoking and drinking, if overdone, are unhealthy . . . and when you do something unhealthy, that's stressful to your body. Shopping is bad for you financially (again, if overdone) and that leads to financial stress. While these things can give you temporary relief, they are not good in the long run.

Once you realize the harm that you do yourself, bad habits become much less appealing. But giving them up still isn't easy because most bad habits aren't all bad. Going out drinking satisfies a need for social interaction and excitement. These desires themselves aren't bad, but we need a better way to satisfy them.

HOW:

Commit Thyself Fully for just one week. In the times that I failed to quit smoking, I was only half into it. I told myself I wanted to quit, but I always felt in the back of my mind that I'd fail. I didn't write anything down, I didn't tell everybody. When I fully committed, I stuck to it. So commit for one week to eliminating a bad habit—you're pretty good at making changes at this point, so you can do it. Tell people about it, and promise to do it for one week.

Know Your Motivation. When the urge comes, your mind will rationalize. "What's the harm?" and you'll forget why you're doing this. Know why you're doing this BEFORE that urge comes. Is it for your kids? for your wife? for your health? So you can run? Because the girl you like doesn't like smokers? Have a very good reason or reasons for quitting. List them out. Print them out. Put it on a wall. And remind yourself of those reasons every day, every urge.

Know your needs. What needs are being fulfilled by this bad habit? Stress relief, comfort, reward, social lubrication, pleasure, love, feeling important, feeling cool? If you're not sure what need is being fulfilled, it's not important to get it exactly right at first—take a guess, and try the steps below. Pay attention to how you feel when you get the urge to do the old habit, and over time you'll start to learn the true need.

Have replacement coping mechanisms. If you need stress relief, comfort, reward . . . what can you do that are more positive activities? I used to do pushups or go for a walk or run for stress relief. A warm bath, a massage, tea, or a talk with a friend are good ways to get comfort or reward.

Not one exception. The mind is a tricky thing. It will tell you that one cigarette won't hurt. And it's hard to argue with that logic, especially when you're in the middle of an urge. And those urges are super hard to argue with. Don't give in. Tell yourself, before the urges come, that you will not smoke a single puff, ever again. Because the truth is, that one puff WILL hurt. One puff leads to a second, and a third, and soon you're not quitting, you're smoking.

Have social support. Join a forum. Ask for help on Facebook. Have a quit partner. Who will be your support buddy when you have an urge?

Delay. If you have an urge, wait. Do the following things: take 10 deep breaths. Drink water. Have some carrots. Call your support person. Post online, asking for help. Exercise. DO WHATEVER IT TAKES, BUT DELAY, DELAY, DELAY. You will make it through it, and the urge will go away. When it does, celebrate! Take it one urge at a time, and you can do it.

If You Fall, Get Up. And Learn from Your Mistakes. Yes, we all fail. That does not mean we are failures, or that we can never succeed. If you fall, it's not the end of the world. Get up, brush yourself off, and try again. I failed numerous times before succeeding. But you know what? Each of those failures taught me something.

THINK POSITIVE. This is the most important tip of all. If you have a positive, can-do attitude, as corny as it may sound, you will succeed. Trust me. It works. Tell yourself that you can do it, and you will. Tell yourself that you can't do it, and you definitely won't. When things get rough, think positive! You CAN make it through the urge. I did. So have millions of others. We are no better than you.

CHANGE 23: DON'T WISH THINGS WERE DIFFERENT

THE CHANGE: *Catch yourself wishing things were different, and let that wish go. Accept things as they are.*

WHY: How much of your stress, frustration, disappointment, anger, irritation, pissed-offedness comes from one little thing? Almost all of it comes from your expectations, and when things (inevitably) don't turn out as we expect, we wish things were different. We build these expectations in our heads of what other people should do, what our lives should be like, how other drivers should behave . . . and yet it's all fantasy. It's not real.

Here's a simple solution: Take your expectations, and throw them in the ocean.

HOW:

Picture all the expectations you have for yourself, your life, your spouse, your kids, your coworkers, your job, the world. Take them from inside you, and toss them in the ocean. What happens to them? They float. They're carried around by waves. The current takes them out, and they drift away. Let them be washed away by the cleansing waters, and let them go.

Start to watch yourself during the day. When you find yourself angry, frustrated, disappointed, irritated, yelling at other drivers, wanting to rant online . . . use these as triggers. They are an indicator that you're wishing things could be different. That you have expectations of how reality should be—that are different than how they actually are.

When you notice an expectation or wish that things were different . . . toss it into the ocean.

Practice accepting reality as it is, and people as they are, without expectations, without trying to force people into the containers you have for them, seeing things as they are. It's a life where you don't need to be disappointed or frustrated or angry—or if you are, you accept it, and then let it go. That's not to say you never act—you can act in a way that's in accordance with your values, and influence the world, but never have an expectation of how the world will react to your actions.

If you do something good, you won't expect praise or appreciation. Let those expectations of reward and praise float away with the waves. Do good because you love doing good, and expect nothing beyond that.

Let the waters of the world cleanse us, and let us walk lightly in a world that is already wonderful without our fantasies.

CHANGE 24: CLEAR A CLOSET

THE CHANGE: *Clear out an entire closet this week.*

WHY: We've cleared shelves and counters and other flat spaces—perhaps even begun to invade a closet or two. But this week, we're going to be bold, and tackle an entire closet. It will feel amazing.

Closets are kingdoms of hidden clutter, lurking in the dark with everything we want out of sight. They can be stressful, not at all peaceful . . . or we can transform them into a little space of peace.

HOW:

Pick a closet to tackle this week. You can start with a small closet, or be daring and take on your bedroom closet. Your choice!

Take a few minutes to scope out the territory. What do you see in the closet? Does it give you anxiety thinking about going through all that stuff? If so, practice letting go of that anxiety. This can be a calming, meditative experience if we let go of the anxiety.

Split the territory into zones that you're going to tackle one at a time: the floor, things hanging from a rod, various shelves, for example. On Day 1, pick an easy zone.

for each zone, the process will be exactly the same as the process you used to declutter shelves and counters in previous weeks: clear out everything in that zone, put it in a pile, sort it into keep, donate/recycle/trash, and maybe box (if needed). Clean out the area of the closet nicely before putting the "keep" items into their new homes, neatly. Get rid of the donate/recycle/trash stuff, and put the maybe box into storage.

Each day, tackle a new zone the same way, until you're done with the closet. Simple!

If you have time left over, feel free to tackle a second or even third closet this week. It's fun.

CHANGE 25: LET GO OF TV

THE CHANGE: *Let go of watching TV this week (including online TV shows/movies, Netflix, Hulu, etc.).*

WHY: Many people view TV (and other similar video-watching such as Netflix, online videos, watching DVDs, etc.) as a necessity. But why? It's not something people did until just 70 years ago or so. Most of human history, people survived without TV. Life was still good.

the average American watches 5 hours of TV a day. Many watch more than that (7–8 hours). Imagine that almost every discretionary hour of our lives are being spent zoned out in front of a screen, doing nothing but consuming. When you subtract 8 hours of sleep, an hour getting ready/dressing/grooming, an hour commuting, 8 hours of work, another couple hours eating/cooking, we have maybe 4 hours of discretionary time (many people can get more than 4 hours of TV because they do it while eating, dressing, working, or they work or sleep less). If we have about 4 hours of discretionary time, we can use that watching TV . . . or being active outdoors, reading, writing, creating, spending time with our kids or other loved ones, meditating, doing yoga, working in the garden, playing music, learning a language . . . you get the idea. TV is one of the least interesting or healthy ways to spend that spare time.

HOW:

This week, commit to letting go of TV/video watching. Think about what time(s) you usually watch TV—this is now free time!

What's something you wish you had time for, something you've always wanted to do but haven't done much of yet? Use this week to do some of that.

If you can, unplug the TV, take away a key cord or cable, and give it to someone else. If other people in your house are watching TV and don't want to give it up, find another place to go while they do that—in your room, outside, to the library, etc.

When it comes to the time you usually watch TV, spend some time enjoying what you've chosen to do. It can be immensely rewarding to spend time reading, writing, playing music, creating in some way . . . spending time with loved ones . . . going outside and being active . . . pursuing your passion . . . cooking healthy meals. Enjoy this time.

All that time you spend watching TV is a huge, huge waste of time. I don't know how much TV I've watched over the years, but it's a crapload. Hours and days and weeks I'll never have back. Who cares what happens on reality TV, when reality is slipping by outside? Time is something you'll never get back—don't waste it on TV.

CHANGE 26: GET MORE SLEEP

THE CHANGE: *Get more sleep this week.*

WHY: Most people are tired all the time—mostly because we don't rest enough. Yeah, I know: duh, Leo. But if it's so obvious, why do we ignore it? Because it's not seen as important as other things: waking early, getting stuff done, attending to a thousand meetings, being sucked into the world of online connections, the god-forsaken television.

So we cut sleep in favor of these other things that are much more important, and then wonder why our energy levels are low. Low energy can have really wide-reaching consequences: our work suffers, we're crankier and so our relationships suffer, and when we're tired we don't have the discipline to exercise, eat healthy, or do the other things we think are important but we never have the energy to do.

Sleep can change all that—when we're well rested, we're happier people, better friends and lovers, and have more discipline and motivation to pursue health and passion.

HOW:

Assess how much sleep you're getting. If you sleep fewer than 7 hours a night, consider getting more sleep. If you feel tired throughout the day, consider sleeping more at night, or taking an afternoon nap if that's possible.

My first suggestion is to take a nap. If you're too tired to take other steps, taking a nap is easy. Even a 20-minute power nap can make a big difference. If you can't take a nap, at the very least disconnect from digital devices.

Computers and smartphones are powerful tools, but being on them for too long tires us out.

Disconnect, get outside, take a walk. Cancel an appointment or two if you can. Stretch. Massage your shoulders. Close your eyes for a few minutes. Breathe.

Exercise. A good hard workout or run, bike or swim will get you nice and tired. A good yoga workout is a wonderful way to do that, as you learn mindfulness at the same time. Even if the workout is early in the day, I often go to bed with a tired body, and look forward to the rest. Don't workout right before bed though.

Get up early. You can get your body to shift its sleeping schedule by slowly getting up earlier. Try 15 minutes earlier than normal for a week, then another 15 minutes. If you get up earlier, you'll be a bit tired during the day, but when it comes time to go to sleep, you'll enjoy the rest.

Go to bed earlier—the Internet will be fine without you. I like to read before bed (a book, not websites) as a ritual that helps me sleep. It takes awhile before your sleeping patterns change.

Establish a bedtime ritual. It takes time to unwind the body and mind. At least an hour before bedtime, start slowing down. Turn off the computer. Floss & brush your teeth. Put away things you were using in the evening. Lay down and read a book (not on your laptop). This kind of ritual helps establish in your mind that it's time to sleep, and your body takes this cue and begins to prepare itself.

Focus your attention. Once you've done your bedtime ritual and unwound, and your body is nice and tired, you need to quiet the mind. My trick for doing that: close your eyes, and visualize what you did first thing today. That might be opening your eyes and getting out of bed. Then visualize the second thing you did—let's say you peed and washed your face, or drank a glass of water. Then you started the coffee but first had to grind the beans. Visualize these tiny steps in detail. I never get past the first hour before I'm asleep.

Sleep is a blessing that I wish on all my friends, all of you included. It's a much-needed rest that helps us to be truly awake once the glorious new day has come.

CHANGE 27: VALUE TIME OVER MONEY

THE CHANGE: *Re-evaluate how you spend your time, and what that says about what you value most.*

WHY: Many of you already have this down, but it's always useful to spend some time giving this some thought. It's about aligning our lives with our values—and learning that money has very little real value if we don't have time for what truly matters.

Imagine spending your life on the things you want to do, with the people you want to be with, giving your attention to the work you love, to playing, to joy and passion and health and love.

Time is our most precious resource, because it's so limited. We can waste it by watching TV, spending time on crappy websites and social media, or we can do something with it that matters, that gives us joy, that helps others.

We can waste our lives away trying to make money, spending even more money, paying interest on the debt caused by our overspending and then trying to earn more to pay for that debt . . . or we can decide what really matters and spend our time accordingly.

When you value your time over money, your priorities shift.

HOW:

Take an assessment of how you're spending your time. What do you do most with your time? Is earning money and spending it a big part of how you spend your time? If so, what does that say about your values?

Ask yourself whether you should readjust things. Make time for the things that you really want be doing—spend time with loved ones, write, create, read, take a bath. You'll never have enough time to do everything, but you can make time to do what's really important.

Consider the direction of your career. Since you spend most of your day working, you better be doing something you like. Is this what you really want to do? Will this particular job lead you to where you want to be? Don't get stuck in a place that doesn't satisfy your aspirations for yourself. Resolve to take your career into your own hands, no matter how scary it might seem.

Change 28: Replace Opinions with Curiosity

THE CHANGE: *Replace opinions that you notice you have this week with curiosity.*

WHY: When we have opinions, we close off all further learning and understanding. We think we know how things are, or how they should be, and so we stop further exploration. This leads to very limited understanding, to a lack of really getting to know something.

We're better than that. We can change. We can let go of our judgments, our set opinions, and open ourselves up to true learning and true understanding.

HOW:

Pay close attention this week to times when you judge others, when you have an opinion on how things should be. This usually happens several (or many) times throughout the day, so you have to be on watch.

When you notice judgment or opinions, see if you can open yourself up to curiosity instead. If you judge someone as stupid or arrogant or ignorant, ask yourself, "Is that true?" How can you find out? Can you talk to the person, give them the benefit of the doubt, try to find out more? When you notice an opinion, can you see if you're right? How can you find out? Explore!

Seek to understand. Try to really understand a person. Put yourself in their shoes. Try to imagine their background. If possible, talk to them. Find out their backstory. Everyone has one. If not, try to imagine the circumstances that might have led to the person acting or looking like they do.

Love. Once you've accepted someone for who he is, try to love him. Even if you don't know him. Even if you've hated him in the past. Love him as a brother, or love her as a sister, no matter who they are, old or young, light skinned or dark, male or female, rich or poor.

What good will loving someone do? Your love will likely only be limited. But it could have an affect on two people: yourself, and possibly on the person you've found love for. Loving others will make you happier. Trust me on this one. And loving others can change the lives of others, if you choose to express that love and take action on it. I can't guarantee what will happen, but it can be life-changing.

CHANGE 29: READ

THE CHANGE: *Spend some time each day reading a good book.*

WHY: Reading a good book is one of my favorite things in the world. A novel is a time machine, a worm-hole to different dimensions, a special magic that puts you into the minds and bodies of fascinating people, a transporter that lets you travel the world, a dizzying exploration of love and death and sex and seedy criminal underworlds and fairylands, a creator of new best friends. All in one.

I read because I love the experience, because it is a powerful teacher of life, because it transforms me. I am not the world's most prodigious reader, but I do read daily and with passion. Lots of people say they want to read more, but don't know how to start.

HOW:

Carve out the time. We have no time to read anymore, mostly because we work too much, we overschedule our time, we're on the Internet all the time (which does have some good reading, but can also suck our attention endlessly), and we watch too much TV. Pick a time, and make it your reading time. Start with just 10 minutes if it's hard to find time—even 10 minutes is lovely. Expand to 20 or 30 minutes later in the week, if you can drop a couple things from your schedule.

Don't read because you should—read for joy. Find books about exciting stories, about people who fascinate you, about new worlds that you'd love to visit. Forget the classics, unless you are excited to read them.

Do nothing but read. Clear all distractions. Find a quiet, peaceful space. It's just your book and you. Notice but let go of the urges to do other things instead of read. If you must do something else, have some tea.

Love the hell out of it. You're not doing this to better yourself. You're doing it for joy. Reading is magic, and the magic will change everything else in your life. Love the experience, and you'll look forward to it daily.

Discover amazing books. I talk to other people who are passionate about books, I'll read reviews, or just explore an old-fashioned bookstore. Supporting your local bookstores is a great thing, and it's incredibly fun. Libraries are also amazing places that are underused—get a card today.

CHANGE 30: CUT OUT SHOPPING

THE CHANGE: *If shopping (online, at malls, etc.) is a part of your usual weekly routine, let it go for a week.*

WHY: Many of us use shopping as a form of therapy—it's comfort, pleasure, reward, socializing, love. We buy online on impulse, whenever we hear or read about something that sounds cool. We think buying things will make our lives magically better . . . but it doesn't. Our lives are the same, but with more possessions to clutter up our living space, and more debt (or less savings/investments).

Impulse spending is a big drain on our finances, the biggest budget breaker for many, and a sure way to be in dire financial straits. It's also a crappy way to spend our time—instead, let's use it for connecting with others, creating and pursuing passion, reading, exercising, cooking healthy food, and learning.

HOW:

Don't shop this week. Don't go to the mall or other shopping area or department store to look around and shop. Go to a store if you know what you need (groceries and necessities), and then get out. Many times people go shopping, with a vague idea of what they want, and get caught up buying much more. Or they go just for fun, as a form of entertainment. That ends up costing a lot. It can really add up. Instead, stay away from shopping areas and find other ways to have fun.

If you find yourself going to an online store, like Amazon or whatever your favorite place is to buy things, stop. Don't go. Make a wishlist and wait a week (or three) before buying anything that you don't absolutely need right now.

When you notice the urge to purchase something that isn't truly a necessity, pause. It's OK to have the urge, but what's important is learning that the urge doesn't control you. Instead, take a deep breath, look at the item you were drawn to, and say aloud to yourself with sincerity, "I don't need that." Then walk away.

Consider extending this a few more weeks if it turns out to be a good thing. Use the time you would have spent shopping on better activities, and save or invest the money you would have spent.

CHANGE 31: LEARN THAT YOU'RE GOOD ENOUGH

THE CHANGE: *Notice when you doubt yourself, and begin to understand that you are good enough.*

WHY: a lot of people come to me because they want to improve something about themselves. They're not satisfied with their lives, they're unhappy with their bodies, they want to be better people. I know, because I was one of those people.

This desire to improve myself and my life was one of the things that led to Zen Habits. I've been there, and I can say that it leads to a lot of striving, and a lot of dissatisfaction with who you are and what your life is. A powerful realization that has helped me is simply this: you're already good enough, you already have more than enough, and you're already perfect.

If you're already perfect, does this mean you don't make changes, like the changes in this book? Well, you don't need to make changes—but part of your perfection is a curiosity about doing new things, trying new things—not because you're satisfied with who you are, but because you like to learn about the world, and about yourself. And even if you're satisfied with who you are, you could do good things for yourself out of self-compassion.

the thing I've learned, and it's not some new truth but an old one that took me much too long to learn, is that if you learn to be content with who you are and where you are in life, it changes everything:

You no longer feel dissatisfied with yourself or your life.

You no longer spend so much time and energy wanting and trying to change.

You no longer compare yourself to other people, and wish you were better.

You can be happy, all the time, no matter what happens in the world around you.

Instead of trying to improve yourself, you can spend your time helping others.

You stop spending so much money on things that will supposedly improve your life.

HOW:

Watch yourself this week, and notice when you have doubts about yourself. Notice when you're afraid to do something—this is because you think you're not good enough. Notice when you're anxious about interacting with others—this is because you're worried about what they'll think, and that they'll think you're not good enough.

Tell yourself: "I'm not only good enough, I'm perfect as I am." Try it, as corny as that might sound, just to see if it sounds true. Does it resonate as something you already believe, or does it not feel right? Do you feel like there are things you still need to improve?

Count your blessings. A better focus is on what you do have, on what you are already blessed with. Count what you have, not what you don't. Think about how lucky you are to have what you have, to have the people in your life who care about you, to be alive at all.

Focus on your strengths. Instead of looking at your weaknesses, ask yourself what your strengths are. Celebrate them! Be proud of them. Don't brag, but feel good about them and work on using them to your best advantage.

Be OK with imperfection. No one is perfect—intellectually, we all know that, but emotionally we seem to feel bad when we don't reach perfection. You aren't perfect and you never will be. I certainly am not, and I've learned to be OK with that. Sure, keep trying to improve, but don't think you'll ever be the "perfect person". If you look at it in a different way, that imperfection is what makes you who you are. You already are perfect—you're exactly who you should be.

Realize that you already have everything you need to be happy, right here and right now. Do you have eyes that see? You have the ability to appreciate the beauty of the sky, of greenery, of people's faces, of water. Do you have ears that hear? You have the ability to appreciate music, the sound of rainfall, the laughter of friends. You have the ability to feel rough denim, cool breezes, grass on bare feet . . . to smell fresh-cut grass, flowers, coffee . . . to taste a plum, a chili pepper, chocolate. This is a miracle, and we take it for granted. Instead, we strive for more, when we already have everything. We want nicer clothes, cooler gadgets, bigger muscles, bigger breasts, flatter stomachs, bigger houses, cars with leather seats that talk to you and massage your butt. We've kinda gone insane that way.

Once you accept that you are good enough, it frees you. You're now free to do things, not because you want to be better, but because you love it. Because you're passionate about it, and it gives you joy. Because it's a miracle that you even can do it.

You're already perfect. Being content with yourself means realizing that striving for perfection is based on someone else's idea of what "perfect" is . . . and that that's all bullshit. Perfect is who you are, not who someone else says you should be.

CHANGE 32: CREATE

THE CHANGE: *Instead of merely consuming, merely existing, become a creator this week—focus on creating.*

WHY: It's amazing how many people I talk to who tell me they want to create a new blog, write a book, start a new business, change careers, make something new. But they keep putting it off.

Does that sound familiar? You've been wanting to do something different, but you don't have the time (or maybe the energy) right now? A million things on your to-do list, a schedule packed full, meetings that keep coming up. You'll get to your Big Thing, but later. There's all the time in the world to do it later, right?

That time will never come. Not if you don't create that time yourself. Seize the bull by the horns, grasp it tenaciously, never let it go. Time has a habit of trampling over us, so softly we don't even notice but so powerfully we become crushed over the course of weeks and years.

HOW:

Create the time. Time doesn't fall into your lap. It isn't handed to you by a kindly old gentleman. You must create it, taking from the world the raw materials you need and shaping it with your bare dirty blistered hands, pushing the clay into form from its shapeless muddy glob.

Say no to everything else. Put off what can be held at bay for the time being. And create time for what is necessary.

Make something. Bring new creative life into the world, change the lives of others, and in doing so, change yours. People in our new world are empowered to express themselves, to create, to become a part of a global conversation and transformation, in a way that has never existed before. What will you do with that? What will your place be in this new, interesting world? Will you have a voice? Will you be a creator, or just a consumer?

Write a book. Or an ebook. Write poetry and publish it on the web. Create interesting, lovely or funny videos, put them on You Tube. Be passionate. Write a web app that will solve a problem in people's lives. Become a watchdog to replace the faltering newspapers. Explore the world, and blog about it. Try something you've always been afraid to try, and put it on video. Be yourself, loudly. Start a new company, doing only one thing, but doing it very well. Start a business that does a service you've always wanted, or that you are frustrated with in other companies because the service sucks. Put your heart into something. Say something that no one else dares to say. Do something others are afraid to do. Help someone no one else cares to help. Make the lives of others better. Make music that makes others want to weep, to laugh, to create. Inspire others by being inspiring. Teach young people to do amazing things. Write a play, get others to act in it, record it. Empower others to do things they've never been able to do before. Read, and read, and then write. Love, and love, and then help others to love. Do something good and ask others to pass it on. Be profound. Find focus in a world without it. Become minimalist in a world of dizzying complexity. Reach out to those who are frustrated, depressed, angry, confused, sad, hurt. Be the voice for those without one. Learn, do, then teach. Meet new people, become fast friends. Dare to be wrong. Take lots and lots of pictures. Explore new cultures. Be different. Paint a huge mural. Create a web comic. Be a dork, but do it boldly. Interview people. Observe people. Create new clothes. Take old stuff and make new stuff from it. Read weird stuff. Study the greats, and emulate them. Be interested in others. Surprise people. Start a blog, write at least a little each day. Cook great food, and share it. Be open-minded. Help someone else start a small business. Focus on less but do it better. Help others achieve their dreams. Put a smile on someone's face, every day. Start an open-source project. Make a podcast. Start a movement. Be brave. Be honest. Be hilarious. Get really, really good at something. Practice a lot. A lot. Start now. Try.

CHANGE 33: EAT REAL FOOD

THE CHANGE: *Replace processed, prepared food with unprocessed, real food.*

WHY: We eat so much processed food these days: chips and crackers and nacho cheese and frozen pizza and soda and sports drinks and cup-o-soup and canned meats and hot dogs and packaged cookies and frozen desserts and microwaveable foods and food from fast-food places. It's filled with fat and sugar and empty carbs and salt, not to mention the chemicals.

Eating real food—as close to its natural state as we can manage—is the answer to weight and many other health problems. Fresh fruit and veggies, beans, nuts, seeds, whole grains that haven't been processed. Doing away with things that have all kinds of added sugars and salt and fats is an amazing way to change your diet immediately.

I don't eat meat or dairy for ethical reasons, but if you do eat meat, you should limit your intake of red meat (many studies have shown the health risks of red meat).

HOW:

Do an assessment of the processed food you eat. Look in your fridge and cabinets—what pre-made foods do you have? What do you eat on a regular basis that's pre-made? Do you eat out at fast food places, chain restaurants? Almost everything in these places are pre-made. If it comes in a package with more than 2–3 ingredients (just peanuts in peanut butter, for example), then it's processed. If it's made of white flour (as opposed to the whole grain, like flourless sprouted grain breads), it's processed.

Put all the packaged stuff in your cabinets in a box, tape it up, put it in a closet or other storage. Get as much processed food out of your house as possible. Don't go to fast-food or chain restaurants this week.

Find 3–4 simple recipes to cook and eat this week based on whole ingredients: fruits, veggies, whole grains, nuts, beans, and the like. Use ingredients you can recognize, not things filled with chemicals.

Drink water and tea, not sodas or other sugary drinks (including sugary and fatty coffee drinks like Starbucks).

Snack on fruits, carrots, raw veggies and hummus, raw nuts.

If you can eat real food this week, you'll see that you'll get the nutrition your body needs, more fiber and vitamins and minerals, less chemicals and bad fats and salt and sugar; be able to eat more without feeling heavy and crappy, and you'll have the energy and nourishment you need to do amazing things in your life.

CHANGE 34: EXPLORE WORK YOU LOVE

THE CHANGE: *Begin to look into doing work that you love (or, if you're already doing work you love, help someone else do the same).*

WHY: One of the keys to happiness—as well as productivity and effectiveness at work—is finding work you love, that you're passionate about. Work you want to do, instead of just have to do. If you really want to do it, it barely seems like work at all.

I've finally found that work, in blogging here at Zen Habits and with writing in general. And I'm just one of many who've done that—there are people all over the world pursuing their dreams, working with passion, losing themselves in their work. Are you one of them? Do you want to be?

the difficult thing for many people is finding what that work is in the first place. They don't know where to start, and it seems a hopeless cause. It's not. You can find that work, but it'll take some looking.

HOW:

Believe in yourself. The main reason people don't try to do work they love, or even look for it, is because they don't think they're good enough. That's hogwash. We've been bamboozled and hornswoggled into believing we are insufficient, that it's scary to fail, when neither is remotely true. You are not only sufficient, you are perfect. Failure is how we learn to get better. It's a step towards success.

Dare to ask. If you don't already know what you love to do, start a list. Do you have hobbies you're passionate about? What do you like reading about? What do you talk about with others? Is there something you always wanted to do but forgot about, or were too afraid to pursue? What are your dreams? Is there something you've always wanted to accomplish in life? Almost everybody has some dream like that, sometime in their lives, but often they don't think it's realistic. Give it more thought now. What are you good at? What are your strengths? Do you have any talents? Is there something you've always excelled at? Write it all down. If you're having trouble coming up with ideas yourself, get help, from friends, family, or a career coach. You may be too close or too afraid to see the answers that are right in front of you.

Take action. If you don't actually do anything, you'll never find it. Start doing research, start making calls, make appointments, take career assessment tests. Take action, now.

Explore new things. Try out new hobbies that sound interesting. Read about new things. Find new ways to explore—break out of your patterns.

Once you find something interesting, pursue it. Read about it. Learn, and try it, and do it, and get better at it. Don't be afraid to pursue it—fear is what stops most people from finding this happiness.

Do a small easy test. Don't think you can start a blog? Sign up for a free WordPress.com or Blogger.com account and do a short post. Don't tell anyone about it. Just write a post. It costs nothing, risks nothing, takes almost no time. But you will learn you can do that one little thing, and if you pass that test, you now know your theory of impossibility was wrong. You can do this with any skill, by the way, not just blogging.

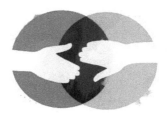

CHANGE 35: HELP OTHERS

THE CHANGE: *Take time each day to help fellow human beings.*

    WHY: Too often the trend in our society is for people to be separated from each other, to be cut off from the great mass of humanity, and in doing so to be dehumanized a little bit more with each step.

    What we must guard against is the tendency of that individuality to have us focused on ourselves to the exclusion of our fellow human beings. The tendency towards selfishness rather than giving, on helping ourselves rather than helping our brothers and sisters in humanity.

    So strike back against the selfishness and greed of our modern world, and help out a fellow human being today. Helping a fellow human being, while it can be inconvenient, has a few humble advantages:

It makes you feel better about yourself

It connects you with another person, at least for a moment, if not for life

It improves the life of another, at least a little

It makes the world a better place, one little step at a time

and if that kindness is passed on, it can multiply, and multiply.

    HOW:

Take just a few minutes each day this week, and do a kindness for another person. It can be something small, or the start of something big. Ask them to pay it forward. Put a smile on someone's face.

    Don't know where to start? Here's an extremely incomplete list, just to get you thinking: Smile & be friendly, volunteer, make a donation, give a gift, stop to help someone who needs it, teach someone a skill you know, mentor someone, comfort someone, listen, help someone take action, buy food for a homeless person, lend your car, help someone on the edge, help someone get active and fit, do a chore, give a massage, send a nice email, show appreciation publicly or privately, donate food, just be there, be patient, tutor a child, create a care package, lend your voice to the powerless, offer to babysit, love.

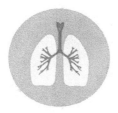

CHANGE 36: BREATHE

THE CHANGE: *Focus on your breath at least once each day this week.*

WHY: Breathing can transform your life. If you feel stressed out and over-whelmed, it can calm you and release the tensions. If you are worried about something coming up, or caught up in something that already happened, it can bring you back to the present. If you are discouraged and have forgotten your purpose in life, it can remind you about how precious life is, and that each breath in this life is a gift you need to appreciate.

If you have too many tasks to do, or are scattered during your workday, it can help bring you into focus. If you are spending time with someone you love, it can help you to be present with that person, rather than thinking about work or other things you need to do. If you are exercising, it can help you enjoy the exercise, and therefore stick with it for longer. If you are moving too fast, it can remind you to slow down, and enjoy life more.

So breathe. And enjoy each moment of this life. They're too fleeting and few to waste.

HOW:

Put the word "Breathe" as a screensaver or desktop picture, as a start page for your browser, or put it up as a note on your wall or fridge or on your desk. Then do it every time you see the word.

When you decide to focus on breathing, take 12 seconds for an experiment: practice focusing on a relaxing breath . . . 2 seconds in and 4 seconds out, repeated three times. That's it. Even that little amount of time can help your body and mind relax. Let your heart rate slow. Let some of the stress slide away.

Now how can you give yourself the gift of relaxing breaths during even your busiest days? One answer is to pair a relaxing breath with an activity that comes up repeatedly during your day. For example, let's say you're a secretary. Each time your phone rings, breathe before you answer it.

If this sounds suspiciously like meditation, well, cast those suspicions out of your mind. We are not here to do suspicion—we are doing nothing. You can breathe, and let go of all that stress and fear, and be grateful for the moment you've been given, the breath that you have.

CHANGE 37: ENJOY THE HABIT

THE CHANGE: *Take a habit you've been working on (from previous weeks), and focus on the enjoyment of the habit.*

WHY: You'd be surprised how many people try to force themselves to do things they don't enjoy. They try to instill "discipline" because they think it'll make them a better person or give them a better life, but what kind of life is it if you force yourself to do things you hate all the time?

If you try to make a habit of something you don't like doing, you're almost sure to fail. I know, because I've tried it many times. If I find myself saying, "I hate this, but I can do it!" then it's an uphill battle, and one I almost always lose. Because after a week or two of doing this, you'll lose enthusiasm. You'll run out of the incredible energy required to form a new habit, and then miss the habit one day, and another day, and soon it's over.

but if you do something you love doing, how hard is it to motivate yourself to do this? You look forward to it. You are excited about it. When you actually do the habit, you're happy, and your overall experience is positive. That's a habit that is much more likely to stick.

When a person doesn't enjoy the new habit, it fails, and when they do, it has a high degree of success. There are other factors, but the most important factor, by far, is loving the habit.

HOW:

Focus on a habit you've been trying to create—preferably one you find enjoyable in some way. It can be a change from a previous week that you're trying to continue or reinstate.

Focus on the enjoyable aspects. If you don't already love the habit, learn to love it. Not by reprogramming your mind to love something you hate, but by finding things about the habit you do enjoy. For example, when I started running, it was hard. I was a recent smoker, so my lungs were crap, and my legs were weak, and I'd get tired fast. But there were things I enjoyed too—getting outside, the fresh air, moving and feeling my heart beating, the beauty of nature, the good feeling after I was done. So I focused on these things, and it worked. And then eventually the running got easier and I loved everything about the activity. This kind of thing can be done with almost anything—look hard for the good aspects, the things you enjoy. If you can't find anything, you've chosen the wrong habit.

Love the habit, and it will stick around longer.

CHANGE 38: FIND SOLITUDE

THE CHANGE: *Find space for solitude each day this week.*

WHY: Finding time for solitude is extremely important, and yet it's an area that is often neglected. I don't mean time alone, where you're watching TV or surfing the Internet or reading or watching the news. Those activities aren't conducive to contemplation, to getting to know yourself, to reflecting on what you've been going through, for thinking about your dreams.

the best art is created in solitude, for good reason: it's only when we are alone that we can reach into ourselves and find truth, beauty, soul. Some of the most famous philosophers took daily walks, and it was on these walks that they found their deepest thoughts.

Just a few of the benefits I've found from solitude:

time for thought

in being alone, we get to know ourselves

we face our demons, and deal with them

space to create

space to unwind, and find peace

time to reflect on what we've done, and learn from it

isolation from the influences of others helps us to find our own voice

quiet helps us to appreciate the smaller things that get lost in the roar

There are many more benefits, but the real benefits of solitude cannot be expressed through words, but must be found in doing.

HOW:

Find 20–30 minutes each day for solitude. Put it on the schedule, and make it the most important appointment of your day. If you don't have a lot of solitude in your life already, it's best to start in small doses of 20–30 minutes at first.

If you're having a hard time finding half an hour for solitude in your busy schedule, here are some ideas for stealing pockets of time from other areas—you can just do them for this week if you like: cut back on television and Internet, wake earlier, go on an email diet, don't go shopping, leave work a little early if you can, or go to work a little late, take a longer lunch, stop watching/reading news, don't do anything after work (cancel other commitments), skip meetings or civic commitments, minimize recreational activities like drinking, partying, going out, playing video games, etc.

During your block of solitude, disconnect. Get away from all electronic devices, including your iPod, mobile device, TV, etc. Learn to fight the urge to turn the TV on or turn your computer on or check your mobile device or play music or read. It's hard, but it's worth it.

Hole yourself up. This can be done in your office, by shutting the door and/or using headphones and the calming music of your choice. If possible, let coworkers know you can't be disturbed during a certain block of your day. Or it can be done at home using the same techniques. The key is to find a way to shut out the outside world, including co-workers or those who live with you.

or get away. This is my favorite way to find solitude, actually. Get out the door, and enjoy the outdoors. Take a walk, find a park or a beach or a mountain, find a quiet coffee shop, find a shady spot to rest. People watch, or nature watch.

Focus on creating, or taking some time to relax, contemplate, take a walk, take a shower, enjoy nature, have some tea.

CHANGE 39: UNCLUTTER A ROOM

THE CHANGE: *Tackle the clutter in an entire room this week.*

WHY: by now, you're getting good at decluttering—you've done shelves and counters and closets. You already know the method. You're ready to tackle a bigger space.

Taking on a whole room can be a bit intimidating for beginners, but you're a more advanced declutterer now. It'll be a challenge that you'll enjoy, and at the end of it, you'll love the clear space you have.

HOW:

Pick a room to focus on this week. You might choose a room you like to spend time in, like the living room or your bedroom. Clearing out this room will make it more enjoyable to be in.

Clear up a good chunk of time each day—maybe more the first day than other days. How much time you'll need depends on how much clutter there is, but an hour or two is a good chunk of time. If you can't find that time, don't sweat it—do whatever you can, whether that's 10 minutes or 30.

Clear a working space, probably in the middle. This is to put your "pile" of stuff from other areas, to sort through. In a bedroom, the top of your bed would do the trick.

Start on one side of the room and work to the other. Do one drawer or shelf or spot on the floor at a time.

Pull everything out of the drawer or shelf (or section of floor or what have you), and pile it in the working space. Clean out the drawer or shelf or floor.

Pick up items from the pile, one at a time, and make quick decisions. You know the drill—there are three options: 1) love and use, or the keep pile; 2) trash/donate/recycle; 3) maybe box, but only if necessary.

When you've sorted through the pile, put back the stuff you love and use, neatly. Note their new homes. Put the other pile into a box to be donated or recycled or given to friends and family. Put the maybe box in storage, as per usual.

Move on to the next drawer or shelf or section of floor. Repeat the process until you've worked your way across the entire room. Do the same thing with closets: one section at a time.

Working like this, you can do a room in a couple hours. If it's really cluttered, it could take 3–5 hours. And it feels amazing when you're done. Now sit back and enjoy the simplicity.

If you have extra time and energy, tackle another room! Or do it in future weeks.

CHANGE 40: ITERATE THE HABIT

THE CHANGE: *Pick a change that you've failed at sticking to previously, and try it again but with one or more adjustments.*

WHY: When we attempt to form a habit, we are using a method (whether on purpose or just haphazardly) . . . and often that method will fail. We can take that and internalize it as a sign that we don't have the discipline to stick to a habit, that we suck . . . or we can just realize that the method was flawed and we need to adjust it.

I call a new attempt at forming a habit an "iteration". It's a version of the habit method, which can be done in so many ways. If you fail, figure out why, and adjust. Try again with a new iteration. The new iteration might work, but if it doesn't, iterate again.

by trying and failing, we're learning what works for us and what doesn't, how to overcome various obstacles standing in our way. Iterate, learn, iterate again.

HOW:

Pick a habit you've failed at recently.

Figure out why you failed. It's not because you suck or don't have discipline. It might be because your routine changed, or it was too hard, or you didn't have time, or you gave in to other temptations, or a significant other got in the way.

Write down your new habit method. This method should have a way to deal with the obstacle that stopped you last time. If it was too hard, make it easier or more fun or shorter. If someone got in the way, find a way to get them on board, or find other support. If your routine changed, figure out what you'll do when that happens again. And so on.

Try the new method this week. Pay attention to obstacles, to your new solution to past obstacles and whether it's working. You're learning what works, so pay attention and take notes.

If you want a habit to stick, start so incredibly simply that you can't fail. Later, you can iterate on the habit until it's at the level you really want. But start easy.

CHANGE 41: HAVE LESS BUSYWORK, MORE IMPACT

THE CHANGE: *Cut back on the busywork you do this week, and focus on impact.*

WHY: We often fill our days with lots of little tasks—answering emails, taking care of small but easy(ish) computer tasks, sending texts and going to meetings and doing errands and lots of other little things that make us feel productive and busy, but don't actually get much accomplished.

We can spend our lives like this, or we can focus on the biggest impact we can have with the time we invest in work.

HOW:

Begin thinking about how you can make the biggest impact on your career or business, on your life, on others. How much impact would you have writing an email (which might help one person) vs. writing a blog post (that might help many people), for example?

Each day, make a short list of 1–3 things that can make a good impact. What will bring in more business over the long term? What will further your career? What will help the most people and do the most good? If you don't know the answers to these questions, it's best to just make your best guess—and over time, as you pay more attention to impact, you'll get better at knowing the answers.

Start each day with one of the high-impact tasks, before you do any busy-work.

Reserve a little time in the morning (not first thing) for busy-work, and a chunk of time at the end of your day for busy-work. Schedule time in the morning and early afternoon for high-impact work. Or find the time when you have the most energy (for some people, it's not in the morning), and do your high-impact work during this time, and busy-work when you have less energy.

Slow down. Breathe. Practice focus. Enjoy the high-impact work. Smile, and be happy.

If you do fewer things, you can do them at a more relaxed pace, instead of rushing to try to do everything within a set schedule. This rule applies not only to your work life, but to your life in general—do fewer errands, chores, civic activities, etc. in order to have a more relaxed schedule.

While many people think that civic activities are high-impact activities (and they may be), the important thing to remember is that you can't do everything—cut back on how much you do overall so you can focus on your impact.

CHANGE 42: DISCONNECT

THE CHANGE: *Disconnect from your computer/electronic devices at regular intervals during the day.*

WHY: This is similar to the Solitude week, except we'll be practicing it in small doses throughout the day. We tend to be connected to our devices—computers, mobile devices, TVs, iPods and so forth—nearly all the time. Our time away from electronics is getting smaller and smaller.

Being connected all the time means we're subject to interruptions, we're constantly stressed about information coming in, we are at the mercy of the demands of others. It's hard to slow down when you're always checking new messages coming in.

HOW:

Set a regular timer to go off every 30, 40 or 50 minutes. I use Mindful Mynah for the Mac, and I've heard Stillness Buddy for the PC is also good.

When the timer goes off, take 5–10 minutes to disconnect. Get away from the computer and all other devices. Take a walk. Stretch. Do some pushups or squats or lunges. Jump up and down. Do a couple of yoga poses. Meditate for a few minutes. Massage your shoulders. Close your eyes for a few minutes. Breathe.

Focus on people. Make a conscious effort to shut off the outside world and just be present with the person you're with. This means that just a little time spent with your family and friends can go a long way—a much more effective use of your time, by the way. It means we really connect with people rather than just meeting with them.

Appreciate nature. Take the time to go outside and really observe nature, take a deep breath of fresh air, enjoy the serenity of water and greenery. Exercise outdoors when you can, or find other outdoor activities to enjoy such as nature walks, hiking, swimming, etc. Feel the sensations of water and wind and earth against your skin. Try to do this daily—by yourself or with loved ones.

Eat slower. Instead of cramming food down our throats as quickly as possible—leading to overeating and a lack of enjoyment of our food—learn to eat slowly. Be mindful of each bite. Appreciate the flavors and textures. Eating slowly has the double benefit of making you fuller on less food and making the food taste better. I suggest learning to eat more real food as well, with some great spices (instead of fat and salt and sugar and frying for flavor).

CHANGE 43: LET GO OF A GOAL

THE CHANGE: *Take a look at your goals, and try letting go of one of them this week.*

WHY: Goals aren't as important as we think. Try working without one or more of them for a week. Turns out, you can do amazing things without goals. And you don't have to manage them, cutting out on some of the bureaucracy of your life. You're less stressed without goals, and you're freer to choose paths you couldn't have foreseen without them.

HOW:

Make a list of the goals you're working towards. Pick one of the important ones.

Commit to letting go of that goal this week. What does that mean? It just means you don't fixate on getting to that result—though you can still do things in the area of the goal. For example, you might still write but not focus on finishing a book by a certain date or reaching a certain number of readers on your blog. You might still go for a run without worrying about losing the weight or hitting a certain number of miles.

Instead of worrying about the goal, focus on the enjoyment of the activity. Get excited about doing the activity itself, rather than ending up someplace in the future.

Put on 'Hey Mama' by Black Eyed Peas and start shaking your booty and get moving. With music like this, who needs goals?

CHANGE 44: TREAT FAILURE AS A LEARNING OPPORTUNITY

THE CHANGE: *Reframe failure, so that each time you fail, even in a little way, you change it from a bad thing into an opportunity to learn.*

WHY: Failure is not the end of something—it's just one of the steps in the beginning. Too often we take failure as a sign that we suck, but in truth it's an important part of the learning process.

We talked about this in the Iterate week, but it can be applied to anything. Did you fail at your last project? Fail to be on time for something? Fail to make your spouse happy? Fail at a class, at reading a book, at learning a language? These are all great opportunities to learn.

Get good at failing, and you'll get great at learning. You'll get good at creating habits, at business, at parenting, at life.

HOW:

Notice anytime you fail at something, no matter how small. Also think about recent failures from a variety of personal activities.

Notice whether you internalize the failures, as a sign that you're not good enough. If you do, reject that idea. It's not true.

Instead, see what you can learn from the failure. Instead of thinking of it as failure, see it as information. What caused the failure? What can be changed? Take notes—this is really valuable info.

I highly recommend that you keep this idea in mind after this week—it's an important shift in mindset.

CHANGE 45: REDUCE COMMITMENTS

THE CHANGE: *Eliminate one or more of your regular commitments this week.*

WHY: One of the best ways to simplify your life is to reduce the number of commitments you have. Commitments are regular, ongoing claims to our time, and we tend to keep adding to them, filling up all of our available time.

the problem is that it's much easier to say "yes" than to say "no". And so we gradually accumulate many commitments, from regular meetings to teaching to coaching to serving on committees and boards to being part of a reading group to working out with people to being in a class or a team or a club and much more.

If we simplify our commitments, we simplify our lives. Let's start this week.

HOW:

Make a list of your commitments—work, personal, civic, etc. It doesn't have to be complete.

Is there a commitment you don't really enjoy doing? Does it seem important but isn't really one of the things on your list of what's most important to you? Start with these kinds of commitments.

Just make a call or send an email, informing whoever needs to know that you won't be able to make the commitment. Just say that your plate is too full, but don't feel the need to over-explain or over-apologize. Your time is important, and you have the right to decide how you're going to use it without feeling bad. And know this: they'll live without you. Their lives will go on.

It's that simple. If you want, free yourself of more than one commitment this week, but also feel free to just do one. Consider eliminating other commitments in future weeks.

CHANGE 46: TURN PROBLEMS INTO OPPORTUNITIES

THE CHANGE: *Whenever you encounter a problem, shift your thinking until you see the opportunity.*

WHY: Every day, we are faced with a number of problems, and how we react to those problems is a large determiner of how happy we are. We can gnash our teeth in anguish at the horrible things that have happened to us, or we can find a better way to deal with the problem.

One of the best methods that I've learned is to find the opportunity in every problem. A problem is only a problem if we think it is. If instead we see it as something good, then it's not going to cause frustration, anger, irritation, sadness. Some examples:

Someone is obstinately opposing your change to become healthier, or vegan, or an unschooling parent, etc. The opportunity is a teachable moment— you can take that opportunity to share why you're doing what you're doing, why it's important, and in doing so, educate others.

Your spouse divorces you—an opportunity to learn how to let go of what you wish things would be, and instead re-invent yourself and explore new things.

You lose your luggage and passports in a foreign country. This is an opportunity to interact with locals, learn their language, surrender yourself to the idea of asking for help, and find your way in a difficult situation.

You're having trouble at work—which is an opportunity to practice gratitude for what you have, including having work at all.

HOW:

Pay attention to the times when you're having difficulty. What is frustrating you? This problem is an opportunity.

When you notice a problem, search for the opportunity. It's there if you look.

Some ideas for the opportunities: the opportunity to practice patience, to remember to be grateful, to meet someone new, to explore a new area, to learn, to get better at something, to work on a relationship, to improve your advancement opportunities, to learn to be passionate, to educate, to let go, to be present, to breathe.

Write down the opportunity, so that it hits home.

CHANGE 47: SAVOR

THE CHANGE: *Savor the little things throughout the day, from food to tea/coffee to being active to nice moments.*

WHY: These days we have an abundance of luxuries, but excess actually decreases enjoyment of life. Sure, we can get massive amounts of rich foods, feasting to our heart's content, stuffing ourselves in alarming displays of gluttony . . . but is that really enjoyable on a regular basis?

Instead, we can learn to savor small amounts of things, and in doing so, simplify life while increasing our enjoyment of that simple life. Savoring life starts with a mindset. It's a mindset that believes that excess, that rushing, that busy-ness, that distracted-ness, isn't ideal. It's a mindset that tries instead to:

- simplify

- do & consume less

- slow down

- be mindful & present

- savor things fully

It's the little things that make life enjoyable: a walk with a loved one, a delicious book, a chilled plum, a newly blooming tree.

HOW:

Start on Days 1–3 with meals. When you sit down to eat a meal, disconnect from digital devices, and just focus on the food. Savor the sight and smell of the food. Take a bite and really taste it. Chew it, savoring the textures and flavors. Really try to taste the different notes in the food. Pause between bites. Instead of scarfing the food down, savor it slowly.

on Days 4 & 5, notice small enjoyable moments throughout the day. It could be a warm shower or bath, a nice walk outside, the sight of the ocean or a sunset, warm sun on your face or grass between your toes. When you notice these moments, pause to really savor them instead of rushing to the next moment.

on Days 6 & 7, focus on the time you spend with loved ones. When you're with them, disconnect from everything else so you can connect with them. Really savor this moment with them, really listen, really be present, smile, love.

CHANGE 48: CLEAR YOUR INBOX

THE CHANGE: *Clear out your email inbox.*

WHY: the beauty of an empty inbox is a thing to behold. It is calming, peaceful and wonderful. An inbox that is overflowing with actions, urgent calls for responses, stuff to read . . . it's chaos, it's stressful, it's overwhelming.

If you have an inbox that's massively overloaded with messages, you need to give yourself some breathing room. A flooded inbox is overwhelming, and you don't know where to start. We'll find a way to get started without being overwhelmed.

HOW:

Create an "actions" folder or label in your email. This is where you're going to store any emails that you need to take action on (other than just replying or filing or whatever).

Pick the most important. Go through your inbox and check off 10–15 that are the most urgent action emails, and file them in this new folder. If you don't get to the sections below right away, you can at least work from this folder for now.

Temporarily archive. Now create a "temp" folder. File everything that's still in your inbox into this temp folder. Everything. You're going to get these out of the way and not worry about them at the moment. We'll get to these, but it gives you a little breathing room.

No more allowing your inbox to pile up. Set a new policy. Every new email that comes in will follow these rules: 1) process from the top down;

2) make quick decisions and act; 3) you must take one of five actions: reply quickly (5 sentences or fewer), put it in your action folder and to-do list, forward, archive, or delete. The one thing you must do in any case is get all the emails out of the inbox.

Unsubscribe from newsletters, catalogs, notices from services, social media updates, etc. Delete them all from your temp folder. Filter out notifications and other things you don't really need to read.

When you have time, chunk through the temp folder, 5–10 minutes at a time. Use the same rules as above—delete, reply, add to a to-do list and action folder, or archive. Feel free to mass delete a bunch of emails you know you'll never need.

CHANGE 49: TEACH

THE CHANGE: *Spend some time each day teaching someone something you've learned.*

WHY: If you've been learning something, there is no better way to cement your knowledge than to teach it to others. It's OK if you don't really know it that well—as long as you're honest about that when you're teaching it to someone.

for example, I'm a beginner at chess, but I will learn something about it and teach it to my kids—they know I'm not a tournament contender, let alone a master, and yet I'm still teaching them something they don't know.

and when I do, I begin to really understand it. Because to teach you have to take what you've absorbed, reflect upon it, find a way to organize it so that you can communicate the concepts clearly enough for someone else to understand it, see their mistakes and help correct them, see where the holes in your knowledge are, and more.

You also help someone with something they want to learn, and in doing so, make their life better. Nothing feels better than this, and it gives your life a great purpose.

HOW:

Reflect on things you've been learning as you make these changes. If you've meditated, started eating healthier, learned to be more present, started doing work you love, etc. . . . these are amazing things that other people want to learn.

Think about others who might want to learn about what you've been learning. Other people might have similar goals, and would really appreciate your help. Keep your eyes open—you might find people who are open to learning with and from you.

the teacher's job, really, is to fascinate the student. Fascination is the key to learning. Then help the student put the fascination into action. As a teacher, you should fascinate the student by rediscovering with her all the things that originally fascinated you about the topic. If you can't get fascinated, you won't care enough to really learn something. You'll just go through the motions. How do you get fascinated? Often doing something with or for other people helps to motivate me to look more deeply into something, and reading about other people who have been successful/legendary at it also fascinates me.

Find a way to be hands-on and do the activity with them. I like to do a workout with people to show them how fun it can be.

Play. Learning isn't work. It's fun. If you're learning because you think you should, not because you're having fun with it, you will not really stick with it for long, or you'll hate it and not care about it. So make it play. Make games out of it. Sing and dance while you do it. Show off your new skills to people, with a smile on your face.

Show them how to learn more on their own. Give them books, websites, a method for learning. But offer to answer questions they might have as they learn.

CHANGE 50: CULTIVATE COMPASSION

THE CHANGE: *Focus on one compassionate act each day.*

WHY: Compassion is one of the few things we can practice that will bring immediate and long-term happiness to our lives. I'm not talking about the short-term gratification of pleasures like sex, drugs or gambling (though I'm not knocking them), but something that will bring true and lasting happiness. The kind that sticks.

the key to developing compassion in your life is to make it a daily practice. Meditate upon it in the morning (you can do it while checking email), think about it when you interact with others, and reflect on it at night. In this way, it becomes a part of your life. Or as the Dalai Lama also said, "This is my simple religion. There is no need for temples; no need for complicated philosophy. Our own brain, our own heart is our temple; the philosophy is kindness."

Why develop compassion in your life? Well, there are scientific studies that suggest there are physical benefits to practicing compassion—people who practice it produce 100 percent more DHEA (a hormone that counteracts the aging process) and 23 percent less cortisol (the "stress hormone").

but there are other benefits as well, and these are emotional and spiritual. The main benefit is that it helps you to be happier, and makes those around you happier as well. If we agree that it is a common aim of each of us to strive to be happy, then compassion is one of the main tools for achieving that happiness. It is therefore of utmost importance that we cultivate compassion in our lives and practice compassion every day.

HOW:

Each morning, reflect on compassion. It can be as you start up your computer, or drink your morning coffee, or take a shower. Reflect on what you did yesterday that was compassionate, who you might meet today, and how you can be compassionate to them and others.

Whenever you meet someone, think about how you can show them compassion. Go out of your way to understand them, how they might be suffering, and how you can help ease their suffering.

See if you can find a way to be compassionate even if you don't meet people—purposefully reach out to those you can help.

Each night, before you go to bed, reflect on how you were compassionate that day. This evening reflection helps you to learn from what you did during the day—what worked, what didn't, why you forgot, how it made you feel, etc.

CHANGE 51: REFLECT

THE CHANGE: *Spend time each day reflecting on the year you've had, and the changes you've been making.*

WHY: a year of attempting changes is an amazing experiment. But the real benefit is from what you've learned, about making changes and about yourself. Spending some time reflecting on those changes and the lessons learned is important.

When you reflect on the changes you've attempted, you can decide what worked and what didn't—what methods of change work best for you personally. And you can decide what changes you want to keep in your life, and which didn't fit as well. Just because they worked brilliantly for me doesn't mean they'll work for you.

Best of all, you can be happy with the progress you've made this year—even if you weren't perfect (don't worry, no one was), you did some interesting things and learned a lot.

HOW:

Each day, spend some time in the morning going over the changes you made this year. Go over the chapters in this book and think about what you attempted.

Take a few notes: what changes were best, which didn't feel as good?

Celebrate your successes! And then celebrate the failures too, as amazing teachers on your journey.

Other notes: what mistakes did you make when you tried to make changes, and what strategies worked best? This will help you learn how to make changes better in the future.

Change 52: Realize You're Not Missing Out

THE CHANGE: *Reflect on the urge to check on things, to worry about what you're missing, and realize that you're not missing anything.*

WHY: Our lives are often ruled by the Fear of Missing Out, or FOMO. (Never heard of FOMO? You're missing out.) Some ways we let the fear of missing out rule us:

We check email, Facebook, Twitter and other social networks often, in case we're missing something important.

We try and do the most exciting things, and are constantly in search of exciting things, because we're worried we might miss out on the fun that others are having.

We constantly read about what other people are doing, and try to emulate them, because it sounds like they're doing something great that we're not.

We often want to travel the world, because it seems that other people are living amazing lives by traveling all the time.

We miss what we don't have, miss places and people who we aren't with.

We work constantly, because we think if we don't, we might miss out on opportunities other people will get.

We feel like our own lives are poor in comparison with the great lives others are leading, and so feel bad about ourselves.

the truth is, we could run around trying to do everything exciting, and travel around the world, and always stay in touch . . . but we could never do it all. We will always be missing something. And so, if we cannot help missing out, what is a saner alternative than letting this fear drive us? Let go of it, and realize you have everything right now. The best in life isn't somewhere else. It's right where you are, at this moment.

HOW:

Pause for just 10 seconds, and notice where you are, what you're doing, who you are, at this very moment. Notice that you are breathing, and how lovely that is. Notice that you can smile, and feel the joy in that. Notice the good things around you. Give thanks for the people you've seen today. Celebrate the not insignificant fact that you are alive. This moment, and who you are, is absolutely perfect. You are missing nothing, because there is nothing better.

Breathe, and let go of all that fear of missing out, and be happy with what you have. Be grateful, and each moment think not about what you're missing, but what you've been given.

When you notice yourself wanting to check social media, email, news, because you think you might be missing something important . . . pause. You don't need to check anything, because you're not missing something important. You're already doing what matters most.

CPSIA information can be obtained
at www.ICGtesting.com
Printed in the USA
BVHW041422170223
658676BV00008B/1463

9 781434 104007